Outside the Lines

Poetry at Play

Brad Burg • Rebecca Gibbon

G. P. Putnam's Sons • New York

These poems are dedicated to my family—
for all the rough drafts
we've been through together.
—B. B.

To
Jonny and
Mum & Dad.
—R. G.

Text copyright © 2002 by Brad Burg
Illustrations copyright © 2002 by Rebecca Gibbon
All rights reserved. This book, or parts thereof, may not be reproduced in any form
without permission in writing from the publisher,
G. P. Putnam's Sons,
a division of Penguin Putnam Books for Young Readers, 345 Hudson Street, New York, NY 10014.
G. P. Putnam's Sons, Reg. U.S. Pat. & Tm. Off. Published simultaneously in Canada.
Manufactured in China by South China Printing Co. Ltd.
Designed by Semadar Megged.   Text set in Agenda-Bold.
The art was done in watercolor and colored pencils on heavy cartridge paper.
Library of Congress Cataloging-in-Publication Data
Burg, Brad, 1944–   Outside the lines : poetry at play / Brad Burg ;
illustrated by Rebecca Gibbon. p. cm. 1. Children's poetry, American.
2. Concrete poetry, American. 3. Visual poetry, American. [1. American poetry. 2. Visual poetry.]
I. Gibbon, Rebecca, ill. II. Title. PS3552.U714125 O98 2002   811'.6—dc21   00-051726
ISBN 0-399-23446-2
3 5 7 9 10 8 6 4 2

Contents

Catch

BLUE SKY

WHITE CLOUDS

HOT SUN

A- BOVE

THE BACK

AND FORTH

OF BALL

IN GLOVE

FRIEND THROWS

TO FRIEND

IN SLOW

TICK- TOCK . . .

THE SLEE-

PY SOUND

OF SUM-

MER'S CLOCK

From way
back here
down
through
the
air
down
down
I rush
to
way
down
there,   then   up   again
up
up
I fly
to
where
my
feet
can
touch
the sky!

Swing

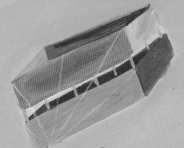

sea!

blue
sky-

last!
at

spring
of
flags
our
fly
we

of that bright
on the waves
way up there
for a ride,
The wind's taking my kite

and look now!
and soaring so free,
and together they're sailing,
they've gone for a glide,
Neither one! They're both flying,

hill,
windy
from this
Now,

or my kite that's been caught?
oh, but is it the wind
and ran out—
as it ran through my fingers, ran up
pulling taut,
and I felt my kite lifting, the string
no doubt!—
But then suddenly, something was starting—

past!"
"Winter's
whispered,
March

breezing by,
out! While
The secret's

And thinking I just wasn't doing it right. . . .
I kept running. And running. And trying. And wishing.
I couldn't get one of these breezes to bite.
I was having no luck with my upside-down fishing.

Cory   **Allison**

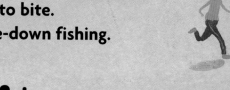

Kites

sky!
and

earth
the

between

tied . . .
perfectly

now is
like our game,
And my kite,

to a standstill, up high.
we have fought
so blue and so wide,
And at last, in our playground,

All right; so am I!
'cause my friend is a fighter.
and we'll fight to the end,
The wind is my friend,

that's all right, I'll pull tighter!
The wind's pulling tight;
in this tug-of-war. . . .
But still I'm not losing

oh my—
or more, and I've only got two—
The wind has a hundred hands,

Emily

prize!
first

day
perfect
this

award
that I

the world
to tell

skies,
blue
than
bluer

like a ribbon,
up there
pinned

kite's
M y

Joshua

Suppose one pops
up left, and high?
And what if the sun
is in my eye?

"Center," Coach
yells, "play it deep!"
But way out here,
I'll fall asleep!

Somehow I feel
today's the day—
at second, I'll make
a double play!

Infield fly or
grounder's hop,
each will meet
one quick shortstop.

Line drive
to third? Will one
get by me? No way,
batter. Come on;
try me.

Not high,
not low . . .
not easy, pitching.
Keep cool—oh
NO! My foot is
itching!

Batting first! It
makes me proud.
(But does Dad have
to cheer so loud?)

I'll catch 'em,
tag 'em, do it
all. And now
I hear it—yes—
PLAY BALL!

I'm in right, and I hope it's not wrong; hope some batters hit the ball long.

Softball

Here's where they throw to, in the first place. If I'm good, it's the best—if not, the worst place !

Tag

Y̲ou're  **IT!**

Look out! Now!

Here she comes!

Let's run. . . .  **Run!! Run!!!!!!!!! RRRRUN!!!!**

Oh!

Which
way?

Yikes! Almost!

Here she . . .

(Not me!!)

comes!

She . . .

 **GOT me! AAAH!**

You're **IT!**  O . . . K A Y .

top.... And
tippy- then
to the I slide
way up and slide
all the ooh what
climb up a ride
until I I slide
I climb and glide
and still I slip and
and climb slide and
I climb slide and
and then slide and
climb ... then I

stop.

Slide

Rolling Downhill

Green
green

blue
blue

green
green

blue
blue

dandelion!
green

blue

green   blue

blue

THROUGH.

hop!

turns
to

take
two

each
foot

stop!
Let

hard
to

fun,
it's

so
much

slow
now—

skip-
ping

fast
or

skip-
ping

go
now,

here
I

right
foot,

Left
foot

Skipping

14

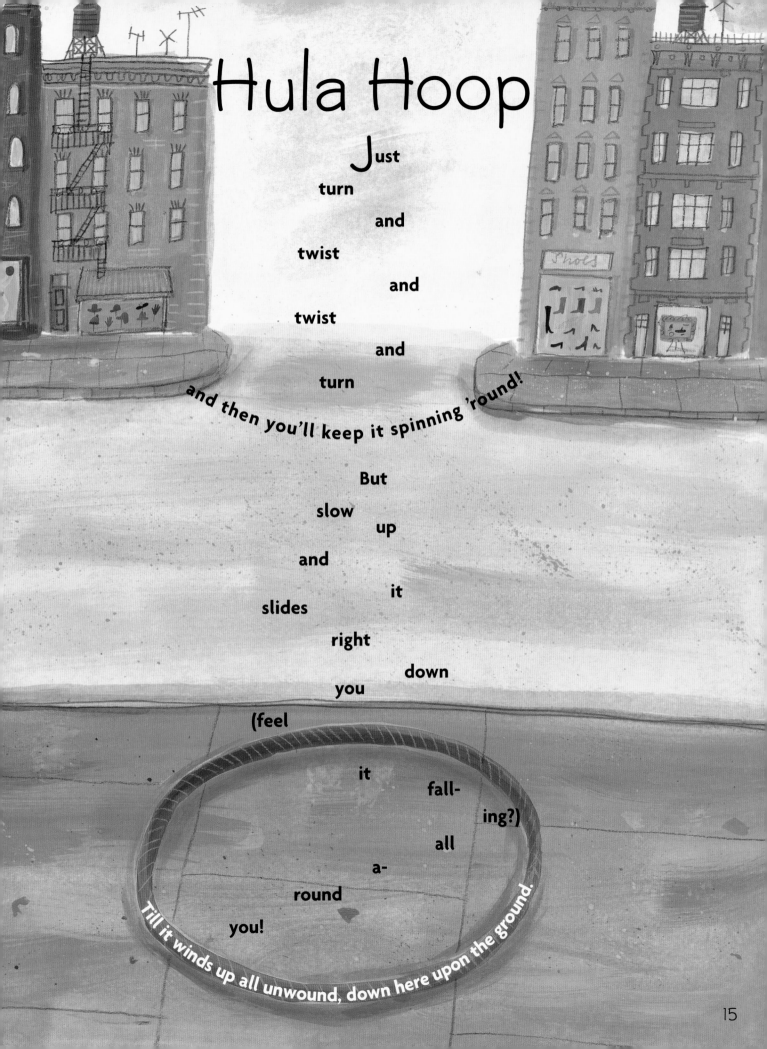

Hula Hoop

Just
turn
and
twist
and
twist
and
turn
and then you'll keep it spinning 'round!

But
slow
up
and
it
slides
right
down
you
(feel
it
fall-
ing?)
all
a-
round
you!

Till it winds up all unwound, down here upon the ground.

Frisbee

hand!

waiting

friend's

my

in

ends

that

planned,

I've

curve

the

along

glide

and

there!—

isn't

that

a track

down

slide

the air—

it ride

to see

I LOVE

And
now
my
friend's
returned
it—
see!
It's
whirl-
ing
its
way
back
to me—
but
I can
catch it,
I know
how,
just reach
out! Quick!
When it's
HERE!
NOW!

dip!

tip

s k i p

s k i p

s k i p

s k i p

Grip

Skipping Stones

Bubbles

Float!

Float!

Float!

Float!

Float!

Don't
stop!

Float!

Float!

Float!

Float!

Don't—

P O P !

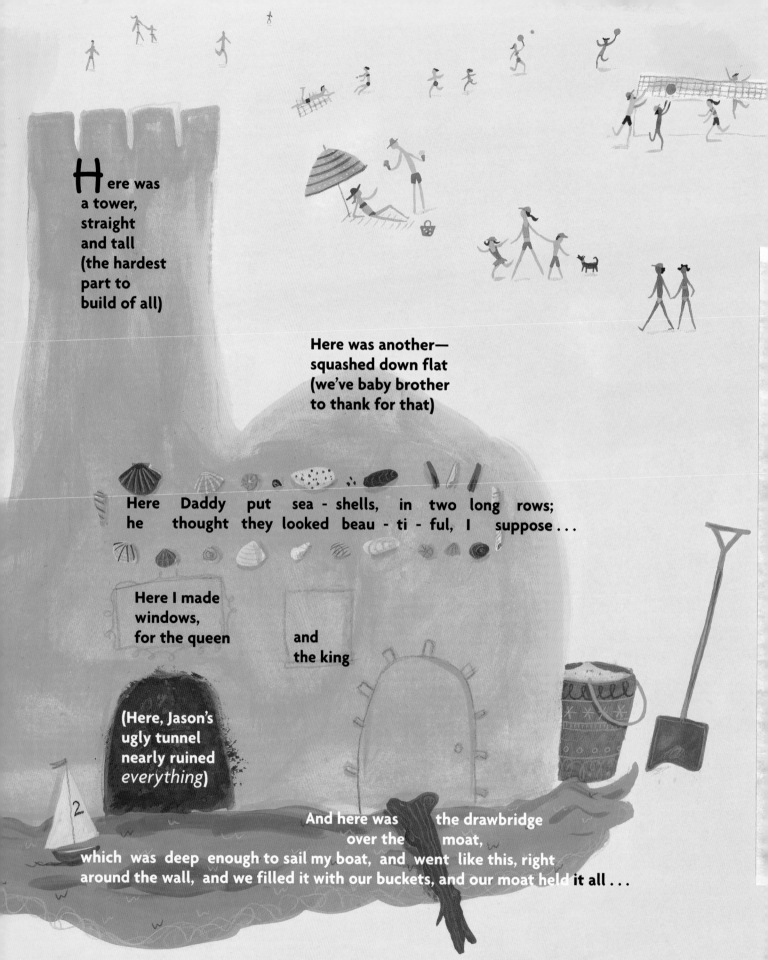

Here was
a tower,
straight
and tall
(the hardest
part to
build of all)

Here was another—
squashed down flat
(we've baby brother
to thank for that)

Here   Daddy   put   sea - shells,   in   two   long   rows;
he   thought   they   looked   beau - ti - ful,   I   suppose . . .

Here I made
windows,
for the queen   and
                                 the king

(Here, Jason's
ugly tunnel
nearly ruined
everything)

And here was   the drawbridge
              over the   moat,
which was deep enough to sail my boat, and went like this, right
around the wall, and we filled it with our buckets, and our moat held it all . . .

20

Sand Castle

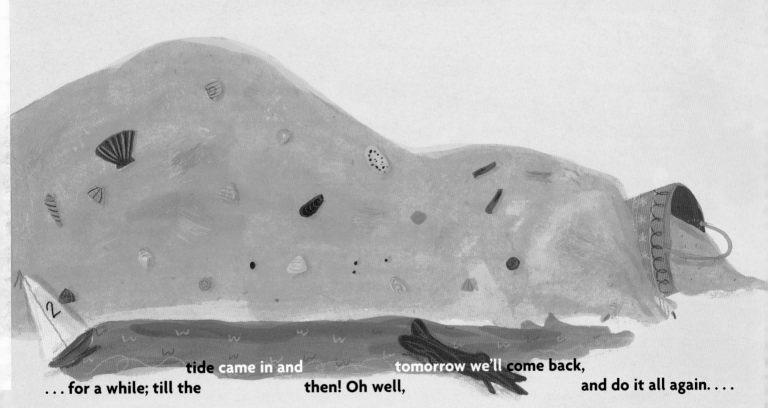

. . . for a while; till the tide came in and then! Oh well, tomorrow we'll come back, and do it all again. . . .

Jungle Gym

Paula's made it to the top

Tommy's leaning way, way out

Anne keeps crawl-ing 'round, can't stop

Joe pushed Mike and made him shout

Mike goes halfway down but then turns 'round to push Joe back again

Samantha's stretched out low and flat

Bobby's al-most fall-ing

Angela has dropped her hat

Margaret's mom is calling. . . .

Fireflies

Blink
here

don't wait!

uh-oh
too late

now where'd
it go?

blink blink

don't know

blink (where?)

DON'T—(blink!)

now THIS . . .
one's . . .

there?

blink (here) . . .
how—?
when—?

blink — AH! . . . Now, then:

Hello, little yellow fellow,
a drop of starlight in my hand;
such a soft and golden glow!
Blink blink blink—

and—

let you . . .

go!

23

Tic-Tac-Toe (a battle plan)

So I hopped up to this corner, drew my 2nd O at the top. . . .

Next, she began. I watched her go with her 1st X overhead.

And that's Then I slid right down to here, *the way* for the 3rd time made an O.

I started here, with my 1st O. "It's your turn now," I said.

I won But I O'd her one more: 4!!! . . . *the war!!!*

She said, "Oh! O!— Your plan is clear!" And her 3rd X blocked my row.

. . . No one had to warn her; her 2nd X made me stop.

Kick
kick,
   kick
kick,
    kick
and
   PASS..

Soccer

BACK!!

Fake—
(right!)

KICK!..

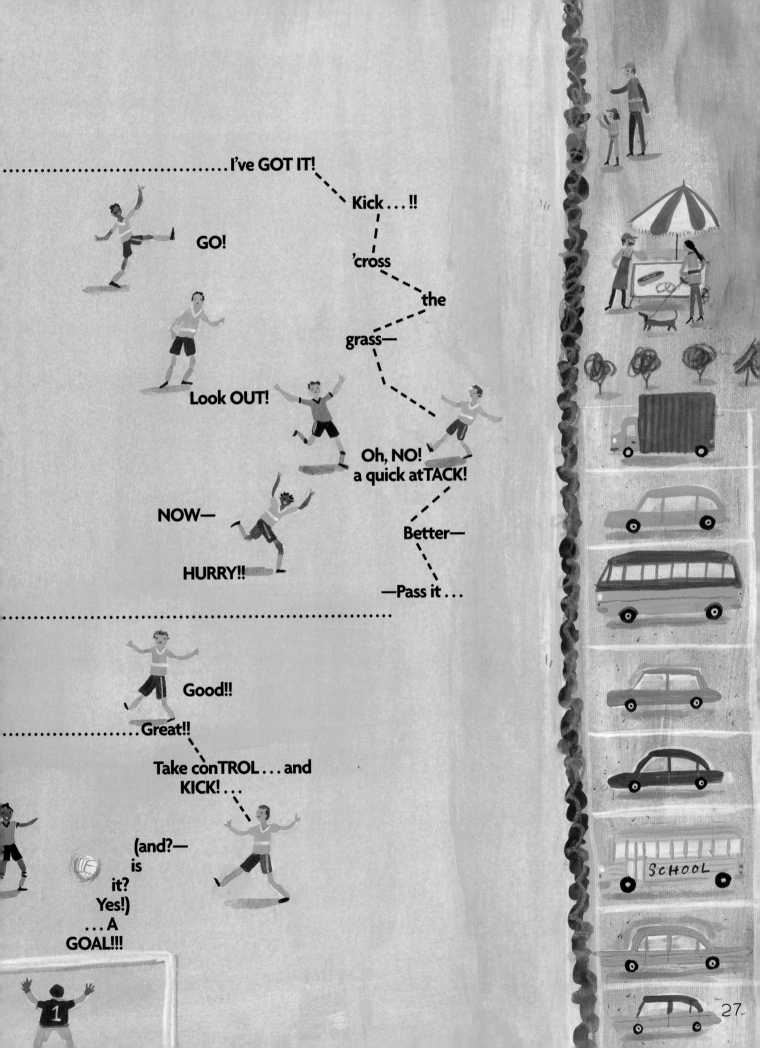

Paper Airplane

I sent
it
smooth-
ly
through
the
air
every-
where
cled
!
cir-
It
But
and
looped
who'd
have
there,
thought
like
up
a
it'd
end
big
white
bird
in
tea-
cher's
HAIR?!

Leaf Pile

L ook out
BELOW!

Look out
BELOW!

Oh yes, we KNOW—
we're not supposed to
jump in here, our dad told us
to keep things neat. I guess he made
that pretty clear ("Don't spread the leaves
all down the street!") . . . but when we see
them piled up high, our legs tell us it's time to
fly—Then something in us spins around, and makes us
race across the ground, and isn't this why leaves start falling?
Just to end up here, and calling, "Jump into this yellow-red, this
crisp October featherbed"—There's just one season for this fun—(we'll rake
them up when we are done!)—"Come dive into this golden heap of happy landings,
soft and deep!"—Next thing I know, we're leaping, all!—and laughing, in the heart of fall!

29

I hear Mom's voice—"No!"—in my head but I just still stop can't my FEET!

Bed-Bouncing

PLETE!

NESS

HAP-

hop-

bed

boun-

on

hop-

'Cause ping this cy is py PI- COM-

Connect the Dots

1. Twin-
15. are!

9. pic-   10. ture   2. kle,   3. twin-
                                   11. poem

14. you   4. kle,
8. a   12. is

13. what
6. tle

7. star,   5. lit-